Kate Fox is a stand-up poet

She's serious about being fu

She's from the North of Eng
time. She thinks it's the pre
will bring. A powerhouse? A

Her second Radio 4 comedy series *The Price of Happiness* was
broadcast in June 2017.

KATE FOX
CHRONOTOPIA

Burning Eye

BurningEyeBooks
Never Knowingly
Mainstream

This edition published by Burning Eye Books 2017

www.burningeye.co.uk

@burningeyebooks

Burning Eye Books
15 West Hill, Portishead, BS20 6LG

ISBN 978-1-911570-09-7

CHRONOTOPIA

CONTENTS

A NOTE ON CHRONOTOPIA

I like the word 'chronotopia' because it sounds like it could be from *Doctor Who*. But also because it describes the place where my poems come from. They come from places soaked in time and time soaked in places. It was the Russian literary theorist Mikhail Bakhtin who came up with a word for this. He looked at chronotopes in literature and art and said they occurred when: 'Time as it were thickens, takes on flesh, becomes artistically visible; likewise space becomes charged and responsive to the movements of time, plot and history.'

Northernness is a chronotope. I'm very interested in that one. It is often talked about as if it's the past – Hovis, whippets, pits – in a way which attempts to keep Northerners there. In their place. Cack-handed attempts at a new futuristic chronotope like the 'Northern Powerhouse' actually keep it stuck in the past because they are full of old-fashioned imagery of men in hi-vis and hard hats pointing smugly at construction sites.

You can find much better new chronotopes in everyday writing and art. I'm a jobbing poet and I'm asked to do it all the time. I've included a lot of poems in this book that were commissions for organisations, and included some information about when and where they were first performed. Quite often the commissioner was saying, 'Make us a new chronotope, love,' but not in quite so many words.

This isn't the most obviously personal of collections, and yet my own abiding passions and obsessions are woven through these pieces which are responses to all sorts of topics. Quarry Bank Mill in Cheshire is a National Trust property which wanted to link the past of its mainly female mill workers with modern issues for working women. I spent an amazing few days in its magical atmosphere early in 2017. I've a few library poems in here and their battle is always to show they're relevant in an age of Kindles and iPads. Glastonbury Festival has a Poet in Residence every year whose job is to draw the strands of time and place together, and I did it in 2013 when the Rolling Stones headlined. For a few years I was Poet in Residence for the *Journal* newspaper in Newcastle. Though many of those topical poems are no longer decipherable, some speak to perennial themes of North-South inequality.

There's a few BBC commissions in there too, including from my *Price of Happiness* comedy shows, two of which were broadcast in 2015 and two in 2017 in Newcastle. The BBC is often trying to show it's connected to place and is broadly living in the same time zone as the people it's broadcasting to. It sometimes succeeds. All this has become more urgent now that the Brexit vote has shown up some of the deep space-time fissures in the UK (and the world).

For me, there is something subversive and powerful about speaking for and from particular, local places. It doesn't have to be parochial. Places at the edges and on the margins need to know they are seen, heard and represented in a neo-liberal, globalised world which leaves many behind. Poetry can do this. Spoken word performed in and for particular places, changing in every show, connecting to the audience in front of it, can do this.

Most of these commissions were to perform the poems in situ as well as to write them. They become something different when they're fixed in a book. But perhaps the book itself becomes a chronotope. Or disappears up its own chronotopic bum. Either way. Enjoy for here and now.

www.katefox.co.uk
www.lasswar.co.uk

CORNETS AND TORCHES

This sunny Sunday, a woman with arm muscles
is uprooting the rusty metal candle holders
from Harrogate's carefully planted park.
We missed the fire garden by a day.
There were just signs about 'Cie Carabosse'
and their show.
We imagine flames from France in the dark,
as we promenade past the rhododendrons.
Usually bandstands are empty,
but here is a real brass band.
We join the families and couples and dogs
sitting haphazardly on the grass.
The bearded band leader says they are from Bradford,
that they are now going to play a Yorkshire overture.
The trumpets, euphoniums, clarinets swell.
I say I like the discordant notes, they are unexpected.
Like Stockhausen or something.
Alfie says they are because the clarinets are going a bit wrong.
I am thinking of my dad's funeral,
a brass band cassette I keep in the car,
Yorkshire Tea,
how maybe Europe could have had an anthem
we could have sung at school.
Taken the mickey out of, but how it might catch in our throat
on a sunny day at the bandstand.
Not an anthem, they'd say. Conjuring goose-stepping. It's dangerous.
We clap at the end, then get up and start walking back to the path
but this next tune's catching me too.
Tears prickling, even though I've not heard it before.
I think about imagined communities,
how myths of Yorkshire are inscribed in me somewhere.
I think of my nan bowling on a Pudsey green and Polos in her pocket.
Her saying, 'Thatcher makes the poor poorer and the rich richer.'
Triggerable but not necessarily in a bad way,
not like I'm part of some sleeping warrior army
set off by the sound of a cornet.
It could be a useful catalyst,
we just need better stories.
Then the notes resolve in my ears.

I recognise 'Do You Want to Build a Snowman?'
We sit down again for the *Frozen* medley.
The clarinets are still out of tune.

THEY SPELL IT HUMOR

*Written at the International Humor Society Conference in
Dublin, a couple of weeks after the Brexit referendum in 2016.*

She tells me to remove my USB stick
so the other presentations can go on the computer,
even though nobody else has arrived yet,
points a chair out for me
and makes to give me back
my coffee cup when I sit down momentarily
somewhere else to put my lipstick on.
Going by her name and accent,
I'm thinking that Swiss efficiency is not a myth
and that that sort of stereotyping is what's got us into this mess.
But when we go over the running order she says,
'I like things to go to time. I'm German, I like efficiency,'
and we laugh.
If you can laugh in your head,
that's what I do later when she says,
'At 6.30pm we issued the participants with the questionnaire,
asking which of the forty-five humour behaviours they had engaged
    in that day.'
My seeing the absurdity of everyday things
would come under 'Amused' in her seven-part schema.
The psychologists talk all day about stereotyping and shorthand,
I meet more nationalities here in a day
than I have in a year for most of my life.
People's phones shine in laps as the eminent linguist
talks about being a maths prodigy and lightbulb jokes.
He wanted to be able to feed scripts to computers
and says that he knows half of a great secret.
Someone in the audience knows the other half
but it will never occur to them to tell each other.
We don't integrate but computers do it automatically.
The Latvian researcher tells us about
Cretans and their image of themselves as lawless and free,
how it conflicted with their other identities as Greek citizens,
and about the crocodile
that was discovered in a lake in Rethymnos.
The authorities wanted to capture him,
but the islanders named him Sifis

and Facebook groups begged for him to stay free.
Apparently in China they don't know the Chinese curse
'May you live in interesting times'
and in Crete, they don't know the Cretan paradox.
Sifis featured on postcards,
posing with a gun in front of the holey traffic signs
they use for target practice.
At night we eat dinner in a wood-panelled hall,
watched over by large pictures of men in wigs.
Later, I compliment my Airbnb landlord
on the portraits I realise are his own work.
I say I feel like I'm getting to know the people in the pictures –
they're alive to me, but not in a creepy way.
He says he's taken a picture of Rolf Harris down now,
he'd photographed him for the *NME* in the eighties
and in three of the frames, when he had his glasses off,
there was a dark, sinister man
with a hard stare we'd never seen on the *Cartoon Club*.
He shows me a computer copy and I recoil obligingly.
It's now captioned with a quote from the trial judge
about how he's like Jekyll and Hyde.
In bed, I read the papers, from a country I don't recognise,
on a screen's glow, glad I don't have to fill in a questionnaire
fitting today's humour behaviours
into one of the seven designated categories.

THE RESERVOIR

Written the day after the EU referendum on 23rd June, 2016.

Families and couples walking round Osmotherley Reservoir,
and us concerned at how low the water level is now,
Norbert scampering through the mud banks,
but one woman with a Jack Russell asking,
'Have they made a beach on purpose?'
The footpath on the other side blocked by metal barriers,
signs saying it's because they're managing the trees
and I look for the twelve stars on the blue background
so I can feel the poignant lack,
but it's just the 'Forestry Stewarding Commission',
another organisation I'd never thought about until now,
and a young Asian couple are lying on a picnic blanket
and a black man and a white woman are laughing at their daughter
peering into the empty stream
and I think that asking them if they're okay after yesterday
would be crass and left liberal heart bleeding
when look, here we all are by the reservoir,
the two lads with their tops off, turning red in the sun,
and the woman telling her daughter
that they won't be going camping for two days
if she keeps this shit up, and the man arcing stones
to the other shore,
and the dad telling his two kids on the other side of the dam wall
to keep their eyes closed and guess which number section they come
    out on,
and I think we don't know anything about each other
until we encounter each other,
really talk here in the dappled light,
so me thinking I could guess who voted which way,
ticking them off as they walk past
is just another dividing strategy,
us here all converging on this point
in the empty moorlands
because really we want to be together,
and we don't know, we just really don't know
and looking is part of the problem
when Alfie points behind us to the family sitting
with their muzzled dog on the river bank
and says, 'Is that dog called Adolf? It is, they just shouted it,
their dog's called Adolf,'
and we both roll our eyes
as Norbert runs on ahead.

14

@ NORBERT SNOOK

Our dog knows that air is memorable and his nose tells truths:
which way the sparrows, shoes and shopping bags went,
that a subtle new bouquet has arrived in the field
where he snuffles grass scents as if they are a fine salad
laid out every morning just for him.
He knows that days are plenty wide enough to greet every being
    who passes
and fixing his brown-rimmed water-bowl eyes on sausages
can bring them miraculously closer.
He knows the dimensions of the last space on the settee,
how to paddle his paws to slot in
and punctuate his flow with easy sleep.
He knows to dash to my feet when he hears the metallic pop of his
    treat tin lid,
the rustle of my coat as I slide it off the hook.
He knows I'm on my way back before I do,
his bottom waggling like a bee high on pollen,
just as excited whether it's been five minutes or five days
since I moved out of his view.
Our dog doesn't know that his days as a quick black cloud will ever
    end,
that repetition is not always the same as prediction,
that his wet pawprints blur metaphors I have written him into.
He doesn't know that I'm not in the house as he thumps his feather
    duster tail
to the sound of my voice on the phone.
That, curled nose to tail tip into an @,
he has become my sign for home.

A DOG OF THE MERITOCRACY

First performed as part of my show The Price of Happiness, about not wanting to be middle-class, recorded for BBC Radio 4 at Northern Stage, Newcastle, on March 11th, 2017.

Yes – class is part of what you inherit,
though if Norbert ever got to Crufts
I'd like to think that he had got there
on his own merit.
Not just because we'd groomed him
for success, made sure his fur
didn't look a mess,
encouraged him to parade
tail-up through the ring,
shushed him during that phase
when he barked at everything,
trained him not to poop
on the judge's shoe.
We do have a chart
containing his pedigree.
On his father's side,
there are champion workers
going back years.
Renowned for their drug-sniffing noses
and prominent ears
(much like the royals).
It's a heritage we can point to
with pride,
though things go a bit weird
on his mother's side.
Not far back in her pedigree
there's a spaniel whose show name
was 'Let's Talk About Sex Baby'.
I'm not making that up.
But we didn't want either lineage
to unduly influence him
when he was a pup.
He's his own dog.
We just provide nourishing kibbles.
James Wellbeloved, rather than Pedigree Chum.
He went to the best puppy school,

we plan his activities,
we wipe his drool
but everything he achieves
will be completely on his own merits.
He could choose whether to be in adverts,
or chase ferrets.
But as it happens
he likes to do pretty much
what his mummy and daddy do,
not including the public nature
of his having a poo.
He socialises, he sleeps,
reads the *Guardian*,
shares our world view.
Due to all those books I read,
he has excellent bite inhibition,
so is unlikely to be subject
to the Dangerous Dogs Act.
We decided not to leave him intact,
so there are no mongrel litters on the street,
no puppy maintenance payments
he has to meet.
He's free to spend the days
sniffing his friends' bottoms.
So, no, I wouldn't say
he's had a head start
just because his daddy
cooks him eggs and lamb's heart.
It's all down to his talents,
and the way they have unfurled,
in what is still,
it must be said,
a dog-eat-dog world.

THANK-YOU JAR

In between a Facebook photograph of a cat riding a bike
and a baby hedgehog piloting a hot air balloon
I see a viral encouraging people to
write down something they're grateful for
and put the pieces of paper into a jar daily,
to be unfolded and rejoiced in at the end of the year
by the time the optimism has run out
like last Christmas's Baileys.
Because gratitude is an attitude.
I pick up a pen, wondering where to start.
Suddenly my heart
is seized with happiness
I was born in a literate society.
I could give thanks for my pen!
Thank you, Mr Biro!
For words, syntax, alphabetics,
for being able to write poems,
avoid athletics.
Then I glimpse my thumb.
Opposable, curved yet chunky –
one of the things stopping me from being a monkey.
Oh, but – there's also my fingernail.
A marvellous miracle of keratin,
protein and dead cells packed tightly in.
And air –
so essential, yet barely there.
Bobbles, Vanessa Feltz,
the polar bear,
my cervix, Velcro,
the taste of Twix.
Now I've started I cannot stop.
How on earth can I decide?
I bet there's nothing you can deride
once you start being a daily thanker,
aggregating appreciation,
releasing rancour.
How can I choose today's greatest gift?
Then how can I best depict it?
I look down at the
glorious glass jar

ready to receive the benediction
of my new gratitudinous addiction.
It isn't there.
Some ungrateful git
has nicked it.

NICE CUP OF TEA

Poem for the 2014 Yorkshire Festival when the Tour de France came to Yorkshire

True grit and Yorkshire?
We've heard it all before.
It's flat caps and whippets
and Brontës on the moor.

It's mills and mines and limestone
and cyclists on the tour.
It's men making this face. *[Makes face of true, manly grit]*

It's Caedmon of Whitby,
the first English poet,
transported to verse whilst looking after his cows.

It's international cyclists
fluent in speed
whilst looking after their calves.
It's not doing anything by halves.

The way we don't like to make a fuss,
we're sensible and stoic,
measuring our life in teaspoons,
our cuppa consumption heroic.

Dunk our inhabitants in hot water,
they're collected, cool and calm,
gathered from round the world like tea leaves
from Poland to Pakistan.

So crash out at a hundred miles an hour
from the blur of the speeding peloton?
No need to turn to steroids
when you can put the kettle on.

You know that in adversity
you're a true and hardy Tyke
if you boil one up and grab a mug
and get back on your bike.

An argument with a colleague?
Your house, your job, your tights fall through?
Say your piece, your head held high,
then have another brew.

Your daughter's up for shoplifting,
your son lives up a tree, you've got leprosy and Alzheimer's
and cancer of the knee
but least said, soonest mended.
Just have a cup of tea.

Other places have their fearsome beasts –
from Loch Ness monsters to yowling yetis –
but you've not experienced the county's mythical strength
until you've joined the queue at Betty's.

If you can keep your head
when all about are losing theirs,
then you'll be a Yorkshireperson –
though won't get far
without a spade to call a bloody shovel
and a lovely cup of char (cheers).

THE DORMANT POET

Based on a commission for Radio 3's The Verb *at the Free Thinking Festival in 2015 on the theme of 'Letting Go'.*

This poem is like a supermarket employee
who has been taught to ask if you've had a nice day
but not to care about the answer.

It cannot let go of some anxiety while you link
a rubber mat squeaking as it is positioned
under spouting water at the top of the log flume,

the suddenly clear view of the road behind you
on the return journey
after the banana boxes have been carried out.

It has relinquished lines
about a dangling string, an outstretched hand,
a dot in the shape of a child.

None of it as effortless
as the daily miracle of the pillow
whose exact moment of occurrence
is evasive as an electron under a microscope.

We've found out sleep is to allow
the day's toxins to flush through your brain
like water through pipes,

interstitial cavities extend
like gaps between words
at the end of a speech,

our limbs splayed
like the branches of monkey puzzle trees.

CHRISTMAS FATIGUE

They started with cut-price cards in January
and presents in the sales.
Carried on at Easter
with the learning of wassails.
In May they wrote the panto
and rehearsed it all through June
and in July they were recording
their charity Christmas tune.
In August they vetted Santas
to check they weren't too weird
and give them a good four months
to grow the perfect beard.
They designed window displays from October
to make sure theirs was the best
and by the time December came around
all they wanted was a rest.

A HISTORIAN LOOKS BACK AT THE GREAT UK WOMEN'S STRIKE OF 2017

First performed at Quarry Bank Mill on January 21st, 2017 (the day of the women's marches against Donald Trump's inauguration).

There was a strong smell of sweat and last night's takeaways on
    the train,
the *Today* programme sounded pretty much the same.
Many birthday cards
were not sent, or addressed to the wrong name.
Of course, the country managed;
70% of managers were men,
except all the schools were shut, all the flights
were grounded and the hospitals open were on black alert.
Fewer lost keys were found, West End theatres went dark,
though most classical orchestras played on.
Kids stared at iPads in office block corridors and hung out in parks.
Bins were emptier, commodes were fuller.
Care home residents stayed in bed,
there was a death spike.
In nine months' time there would be a birth rate dip, a divorce peak
and they'd have to recruit hundreds of new counsellors for Relate.
Fewer doctors gave hugs, there was a rise in falls
and elderly people craved touch.
Diet clubbers went unweighed, appointments unkept and unmade.
Nearly half of academic staff were off, but not quite 20% of professors.
Supermarket checkout lines snaked out of stores,
Babestation Live screened reruns of *Match of the Day*,
employers saved 20% less pay than if men had struck.
Hair looked bad, many wore hats.
Some men discovered vacuuming is relaxing, there was no waxing.
71% of MPs were working, though they made their own tea,
and couldn't hear themselves for babies screaming on green leather.
90% of executive directors were men and met at conference tables
stained with coffee rings,
where they spoke 100% of the time
(instead of the 75% studies showed was the norm in mixed-gender
    meetings back then).

Few people taught yoga, dance or lifesaving. Nobody was born.
Nothing much happened with towels, bedding or curtain rings.
This commissioned poem was never fin—

HIPSTER MAN

Hipster man, hipster man,
even your art is artisan.
Your internet start-up might make you rich,
you eat Coco Pops ironically
in your flat in Shoreditch

Hipster man, hipster man,
you're a *Star Wars* fan,
you have no gears on your bike,
your name is probably not Derek or Bob or Mike.

Hipster man, hipster man,
you can make quinoa flan (and pronounce it),
your moustache is waxed,
your Mini Cooper's taxed.

Hipster man, hipster man,
your underpants match your camper van,
you inadvertently cause house price rises,
you wear skinny man jeans in skinny man sizes.

Hipster man,
you're in the know.

Hipster man,
your pumps are retro.

Hipster man,
you're bringing vinyl back.

Hipster man,
culture's reversed.

Hipster man,
I heard of you first.

JOE AND THE ANIMALS

One of the poems from the 'Home and a Job' project run by Youth Homelessness North East. Participants shared their experiences of benefits sanctions leaving them unable to eat and a job centre that treated them like 'shit on a shoe'. They all just wanted a home and a job.

I like getting chased by animals.
A cow used to chase us round Bolam Lake.
I used to build treehouses, wander round looking for things.
How did I go from a house at Bolam Lake to somewhere as low as
    here?
We ran round for three hours once just chasing a fox.
We made a video.
Everyone in Ponteland's slithering snakes.
In town, people of all ages are your pals.
I sit there at night, wide-eyed,
looking round like an owl.
I know what to do at night, I'm in control.
Or I'm a bat, flitting. Flying round random places, having a laugh.
Then sleeping.
There's more to notice at night.
I can concentrate more.
It's quieter but there are still surprises.
I like small places, a cupboard rather than a room.
I'm a badger, wandering round at night,
black and white.
You don't want to mess with a badger.
They flip good and are calm after.
I run through hundreds of situations in my head,
always calculating.
I'm cunning as a ferret. Getting away with things
without being caught.
I like blank things you can do stuff to.
One day I could be a greyhound. Fast but calm.
I want to be calmer.
I'll live in a field.

I'M INVISIBLE TO THE DAILY MAIL

I'm invisible to the *Daily Mail*.
I could walk past them going,
'Oooooooh, look at me, look at me,'
and they still would not be able to see.
I am not a ball in a game of *Daily Mail* bingo.
It will not say that I'm
giving a glimpse of flesh,
just covering my chest in a flirty frock,
showing off my toned beach body,
revealing too much in a daring photoshoot
they just happen to have reprinted,
shot by shot.
I'm not blessed by fame,
so they're not interested
in my makeup-free shame,
how I went out looking frumpy,
then got dumped 'cause I was dumpy,
haven't had any Botox which left
me looking like 'A New Woman!'
or a Badly Stretched Balloon,
I didn't 'let myself go' after childbirth
or 'snap back into shape' amazingly soon.
I'm not an 'abandoned woman'
or a 'yummy mummy'.
I have a rounded tummy
but am not pregnant.
I'm carrying three extra stone
which will not repopulate the world.
(Well – unless my fat was removed by liposuction,
I had that long-awaited breast reduction
and the excess fed to people without enough fat in their diet.
That *Apprentice* winner should try it
in one of her clinics.)
They couldn't say my breasts have ballooned, sagged,
or been tragically cut off,
thus depriving a baby of its rightful dinners.
I'm invisible to the *Daily Mail*,
though I'm pretty sure I am real.
I wear this invisibility cloak
because my body's not connected to a bloke.

It's not obviously shouting sex,
getting a Hollywood star to chuck off his keks,
it's not doing its duty as a mother,
it's just some sort of corporeal Other.
I'm invisible to the *Daily Mail*.
I don't see this as a fail.
I'm definitely here;
they cannot make me disappear.
If they won't see me, that's just tough –
I'm going round their office
to nick all their stuff.

COULD'VE

First performed during my show about not wanting children, the first in my The Price of Happiness *series, recorded for BBC Radio 4 at Live Theatre, Newcastle, March 2015.*

You could've been a contender or con-artist.
You could have cured kippers or cancer.
You could've been a line manager or dancer.

You could have split hairs or the atom,
you could have had black hair or heads
you could have put up resistance or sheds.

You could have taken chances or the mickey,
you could have saved whales or penny pieces,
you could have thrown pots or faeces.
You could have given me haemorrhoids
or a reason to live,
driven me mad or in cars,
been into serial killers or bars.

You're consequence-free as a midnight idea,
a walletless trip to Ikea.
You're a blank page,
perfect as the job I'll never apply for,
an empty stage,
the unrequited love I'll never try for.

You're the pill I never swallowed,
and the one I did.
You're instructions never to be followed,
a sealed bid.
An undelivered message,
embryonic, untapped, free,

and inextricably
part of me.

TEN WAYS TO BE NORTHERN

Inadvertently

What a lovely spa, with such gorgeous Peruvian lute music. The steam arising from the hot tub like a cloud of wellbeing. My sinews relaxing like a cello after a concert. The menu brought on a velvet cushion. Seven pounds for a teabag and hot water – how much?!

Ingratiatingly

I fully understand the challenges faced by this region after the loss of industry. However, there's a bright future in renewables ahead. My father, who was from Yarm, often spoke of his deep, abiding love for the region. He would show us pictures of it as it was in 1952, when he last travelled north of the Watford Gap.

In attempted working-class solidarity

These Southerners don't really get it, do they? I mistook the hummus for the halloumi and not one of them laughed. They just don't have the same sense of humour as us – or hummus.

Internally

I may have the voice and spirit of a soft Southerner, but inside I have the heart and stomach for black pudding of a Northerner through and through. Watch me cry when Leeds lose, watch me.

In relation to coats

If you don't take your coat off now you're inside you won't feel the benefit.

A coat? No need, I'm hard, I don't need coverings. In fact, I only keep my skin on to be polite.

In language

The pot's calling the kettle grimy arse, you'll never learn while I piss in your ear and don't leave me sitting here like Venus on a rock bun.

Infamously

Zayn Malik's from Bradford, you know, and Delius. The Spiders on Mars came from Hull and David Bowie's dad was born in Doncaster. Sting's dad used to be our milkman.

Intermittently

I get very Northern on the phone to my mum, and when I eat fish and chips. But I'm not very Northern at work or in the bath, I don't think. I'm more Northern in the South than the North.

Inadequately

For viewers who were distressed by our raw depictions of Northern English in its natural habitat, we would like to apologise. In future we will be adding warnings and subtitles. Try think of these programmes as similar to the latest Scandi-drama on BBC Four – cool in its Otherness. Bags be first in the queue for ironically worn flat caps.

Interrogatively

Alreet, pet?

I DO SOLEMNLY SWEAR

A Verb *poem recorded in Manchester on the day of the* Brexit *referendum*

I do solemnly swear
that I do sometimes swear in place of a full stop,
or a 'very',
or to convey that I'm really rather angry indeed,
or that I want an audience to laugh
at the end of this sentence.
This flaming sentence, you twunts.

I do solemnly swear
more often than frivolously,
because words are things to me
and swearwords are bullets
compared to the safety nets
of words which point beyond themselves.

I do solemnly swear that,
compared to Bernard Manning,
I'm not a conscientious objector,
it's just I can't pull the fu— the fri— the flippin' trigger,
even though comedy's no longer war,
just team building
with paintball guns.
But it's the look on the faces
of the ones you hit,
it's my brain
failing to take it as a game,
like my atheist gut
receiving bread as if it's Jesus.
My body believes everything you tell it,
sticks and stones
can break my synapses.
But the comedian weighed down by swearing
is like a heavy metal singer
who says power chords go right through them,
an architect
who is freaked out by the indeterminacy of doors,
a doctor who can't stand the sight of... queues.

I do scientifically swear that,
if I was wired up to electrodes
to measure electrical conduct through your skin,
I wouldn't be breaking a chuffing sweat,
as euphemisms cannot reproduce the real effect;
pretend swearing is poor conduct.

I do historically swear that
swears are social distinctions made flesh,
the ghosts of rules
about what we cannot name:
God's parts in vain,
bodies,
even mentioning trousers
was once considered deeply profane.

I do regretfully swear that the
biggest blooming modern taboo
is believing you
are superior to others.
There are discriminatory words
I cannot even say in my head.
Do not think of elephants.
What if we all thought of the worst
word we could say right now…?
It would pass broadcast compliance
despite the internal violence
of our shared subversive silence.

You honey drizzler,
you Cath Kidston print garlic crusher!
Swearing is class!
I mean swearing actually is class!
No wonder, as someone who came of age
in John Major's classless Britain,
into the meritocracy myth,
I struggle,

though I do Northernly swear
that flat-vowelled vernacular

is chuffing spectacular!
Telling somebody
where you live
can sound like a curse:
Cleckheaton!
Heckmondwike!
Mother Hubbard,
you barm cake,
Terry Christian on a bike!

I do swear in a post-Cartesian manner
that it has the power to collapse
the mind-body duality,
create a new reality.

No word is inherently dirty or clean,
a lexicon is not a laundry list,
old taboos are washed away,
we uncover ones we'd missed.

I do Shakespearianly swear
that profanity is not separate from literary merit:
you scullion,
you rampallian,
you fustilarian,
William did it right,
cream-faced loon,
hunchbacked toad,
the Bard wasn't beeping polite.

Ah.
Asterisk me,
bleep me,
there's so much to erase,
quieten these words in our ears,
fade them from our gaze.

I do, in conclusion, swear that it is cathartic,
drops barriers,
builds offence,

non-verbal as pure music,
punctuation,
onomatopoeic recompense.

Your heartbeat can speed
as words shift place and time,
your blood quicken in anticipation
at a suspended rhyme,
so I'll end with a final oath
amid this innuendo and farce:
I consider both swearing and poetry
to be a right load of –
performative language which paradoxically both heightens and
reduces stimulation while relationally enacting social divisions
and the parameters of what it is possible to say and not say in
everyday discourse.

TWO WOMEN SWIMMING BREASTSTROKE IN THE POOL

There are two women swimming breaststroke in the pool,
ploughing slowly, firmly, up and down,
there are two women talking as they swim
in every pool, in every town.

They're in no rush, they will not push,
they're immersed in what they have to say,
these two women, conversing and abreast,
sailing on, in their stately way.

There's always two women swimming breaststroke
in the pool,
they're not afraid to breathe and take up space,
these two women with their heads above the water
bend the rest of us to their glacial pace.

No one can pass them, swimming breaststroke in the pool,
a tidal barrier clocking up the lengths and miles,
woman-spreading across the lane,
low voices echoing off the tiles.

There's two women swimming breaststroke in the pool,
they give me pause, they slow me down.
But when I'm behind the women swimming breaststroke in the pool
I sometimes wish they'd fucking drown.

THE EVOLUTION OF THE GEEK

In sixteenth-century Germany fairground workers who bit the
heads off live chickens were called 'gecks' – which meant 'fool'
or 'simpleton'.

Maybe you're a linguistic geek,
ever ready with a grammatical tweak?
Or an etymological geek, one of those nerds
always digging for the origins of words.
'Geek' came from the German for 'fool'
back before anyone wore T-shirts
announcing geeks were cool.
Millions of years earlier
when humanity's lot looked dire
it took a geek
to stick at rubbing a stick against another stick
long enough to discover fire.
She shouted, 'Live long and prosper,
without me you'd be dead!'
Another geek whittled for ages
to fashion the first arrowhead.
Even he thought this effort was daft,
little knowing he'd just discovered
World of Warcraft.
The summer everyone went mad for rolling log races,
a tribe's resident geek pointed out they could use this
for transport to far-off places.
She didn't have much skill
at knowing how people feel,
but she'd go down in history (or not)
as the inventor of the wheel –
and Cadbury's Mini Rolls.
Arabic geeks with abacuses,
Greek geeks like Pythagoras who,
alongside baking geek Mary Berry,
revealed why
the world is better with infinite pi.
The first Apple geek was, of course – Isaac Newton.
Others discovered plants, planets, its and IT,
built bridges, fridges, designed the first nightie,
and still had time to complain about inappropriate uses

of the Comic Sans font.
It's not what you know
when knowledge is ever-growing
but what you know about one thing.
Geeks thrive in a world of specialism;
even now one will be writing an algorithm
to calculate their net worth
and predict exactly when the geeks
will inherit the earth.

TOO OLD

Too old to fancy Justin Bieber,
too old to still get spots,
too old to be bored by the news,
too old to drink vodka shots.

Too old to wear Doc Martens,
too old to say OMG,
too old to shop at Top Shop,
too old to watch BBC Three.

Too old to drive a Beetle,
too old to go on the swings,
too old to nip your sister,
too old to wear fairy wings.

Too old to forget to say thank you,
too old to still like pink,
too old to go 'Ner-ner-ner-ner-nuh!'
Too old to puke up after too much to drink.

Too old to go camping for the first time,
too old to learn new names,
too old to be wearing hot pants,
too old to watch *The Hunger Games*.

Too old to read *NME*,
too old to have candles on your cake,
too old to eat Pot Noodles,
too old to swim naked in a lake.

Too old not to pack a cardie,
too old to drink through a straw,
too old for a single bed,
too old to know what the Kardashians are for.

Too old to cry at a bus stop,
too old to believe that life is fair,
too old to care what other people think
of what you do or what you wear.

Too old to give up easily,
too old to still be told,
too old to act your age
or believe there's any such thing
as being too old.

THE RADICAL LOLLIPOP LADY SPEAKS

I have the power to stop traffic;
I do not need a push-up bra to do it.
All who cross here are equal.
My intersection will be feminist
or it will be bullshit.

UKIP

A chain of low-budget hotels
is what Ukip sounds like it should be.
Nigel Farage as manager
and owner and maître d'.

Greeting you at reception,
pint in hand, then serving at the bar,
scrubbing away the dirt
and helping you park your car.

Sometimes guests worry he's everywhere;
where's his staff and where's his spouse?
Until they realise he's the only one
who can be trusted front of house.

It started off distinctively;
its offer gets ever-uniquer,
serving British grub like tiramisu,
pilau rice and chicken tikka.

Union Jacks are everywhere.
This national identity thing is hard work.
The hotel serves kebabs on April the 23rd
since St George was actually a Turk.

Godfrey Bloom's in charge of housekeeping,
though today the kitchen is shut,
and the head chambermaid resigned yesterday
after he called her a slut.

Jeremy Clarkson's very welcome here,
he's just the sort of friend they want to make,
though it's always a little bit stressful
worrying whether he'll like his steak.

The Ukip Hotel say they're definitely not racist at all,
hoped Lenny Henry would do their TV ad,
but he's already sold out to the Premier Inn.
A few of the staff were secretly glad.

There is a high staff turnover,
a few caught with their hands in the till,
they have to get two people now
to sign off everyone's bill.

They've got doctors always on hand,
though if guests need them they've got to pay,
but having healthcare is surely worth
that extra ten quid a day.

Some of them come from abroad,
because we've not got enough medics trained over here,
and the bedside manner's the same
whether they're from Coventry or Korea.

It's been harder than the hotel ever imagined
to get people to make a bed or scrub a bath.
They really meant to employ British
but they just couldn't get the staff.

They're very pleased with the Poles,
and the Romanians who've spent years in the area,
though they never had that flood
of people they expected to come here from Bulgaria.

They've employed some foreign students,
instead of the expected EU influx,
though they're not very popular with guests
with their cleverness and their heads in their books.

And the way they say that immigrants
bring in twenty billion more pounds than they actually take out,
and other inconvenient facts
which cause temporary Ukip guests to doubt.

So it's certainly quite a difficult period
for the venture that is the Ukip hotel.
Even with Nigel Farage doing everything,
business isn't going that well.

Some say there are too many immigrants
and they're fed up of the rain,
so they're going to close the whole thing down soon
and all go and move to Spain.

.

THE WORD 'PURGE' IS TOO LATIN

There are simply too many foreign words
coming over here,
taking our words' jobs and dictionary places.
It should not be taboo
to say this.
Except we won't be saying taboo –
it's Hawaiian.
It is absurd –
though there's a French word
we can also easily replace.
I can simply say this contamination
is a disgrace,
this centuries-old linguistic invasion.

What have these words really contributed anyway?
Yes, contributed is French
but I could just as well say
given.
I don't have to use the Indian juggernaut
when I can say a truck has been driven
through our way of life.
Finding good solid homegrown words is a breeze.
Except that's Portuguese.
I mean, it's easy.

We'll rename the party,
since Conservative is French.
These verbal invasions just aren't cricket any more.
We'll be calling that 'bat and ball' in future,
since cricket's Dutch,
and telling Johnny Foreigner where to stick it.
We need to put their words on the bench.
Though we'll call him Johnny something else,
since foreigner and alien are also French.

We're sending joy, imagination, generosity and humanity
back too – they're welcome to them!
As if we wanted nuance and mix anyway.
Last seen behind barbed wire staring out across the Channel.
Tolerance? Let's repatriate that today.

I'm sure we can find other things to say.
Managing without money is not a bind.
There's always another word you can find,
though not loot because that is Indian.
Sugar.
No, that's Indian too.
I mean shoot.

You'll see, we'll still dominate the cultural landscape,
though not in so many words
as dominate and landscape are Dutch.
But you can't touch us.
It's poppycock to say we'd struggle.
Though goodbye, poppycock,
which comes from pappekak,
Dutch for soft dung.
Anyway, we'll still have plenty of words left
to run
the NHS. Though not medicine
(French again).
We'll call it something else,
no fuss.
Like the Hungarian coach – we've still got bus.
Arabic sofa's out – easy, we'll all say settee.
Shampoo's Indian, say hair wash and be free.
Chocolate's Spanish – cocoagloop is fine with me.
Who wants to say alcohol, chemistry or admiral anyway?
Those Arabs are welcome to their verbal fetters.
We don't need those saucy French letters –
so mammary, sex and erection can go
and the Italians can get off on their own dildo.

What we need in this country is homegrown word wealth,
our very own dictionary moguls.
Though we'll need a new word for them too, please.
And who knew tycoon was Japanese?

Bugger.
Enjoy that too – it's Turkish.
Look, I don't really care,

47

we don't need those foreign dicks
to help us swear.
Though there's another we'll have to turn in
as, unfortunately, bastard is German.
Like Old English itself, really,
but we need to focus on the future,
not the past, clearly.

It's time to go home,
venture, serendipity and marmalade.
You've outstayed
your welcome.
I'm fine with shredded orange on toast.
Once we've found a new word for orange,
which is Indian.
Well, it's about time.
Though that reminds me,
the French will be reclaiming poet and rhyme.

No more unBritish rubbish in newspapers
and magazines,
which we'll have to call periodicals from now on.
Don't think anyone's going to miss
coffee, logic and scrutiny when they're gone.

It is scaremongering
to say that simply pointing out that these words
don't belong here
could lead to violence.
Let them leave quietly.
Enjoy the silence.
Which will also have to change its name.
You can't call this a purge,
as that's from Latin.
Well, no more.
No more.
It's time we took our language back,
that much is clear.
And, as it's Arabic,
no one can say
we have reached
a cultural nadir.

THE DAY OF THE HIJAB

To the First Story writing groups at Feversham College, Bradford, from whom I learned so much across three wonderful years, 2013 to 2016.

1.

I've heard a lot from white people like me
about what Muslim women wear –
Have you seen how they're dressed?
And by the way they're all oppressed,
but I haven't heard quite as much
from Muslim women,
so I was not going to add any more words
when there's plenty going spare.
It isn't that I don't care;
I just wasn't sure what I had to share.
Then Naaila asked me to dress in a hijab for a day,
but I still worried my views would be in the way.
Facebook friends said I'd be a cultural tourist,
patronising, making it all about me,
Muslim women's views are the ones we need to see
and have you seen the way they're dressed?
And by the way they're all oppressed.
I've run a writers' group with teens
at a Bradford Muslim girls' school;
we didn't talk about their hijabs for a year,
until pretending not to notice them
came to seem almost cruel.
Friends would say,
Have you noticed how they're dressed?
And by the way they're all oppressed
and I'd think they spoke more than girls
I'd worked with in unsegregated schools,
where the presence of boys competing to speak
means silence becomes one of Year Nine and Ten girls'
many unspoken rules,
and I knew the Feversham girls have plans for their futures,
are articulate and funny
and sometimes have schemes for how
poets like me could manage to make more money

and, yes, I'd seen the way they're dressed,
but I wasn't sure they were all oppressed.
Then on a trip out to Huddersfield University
one of the girls said ruefully their blue scarves
made them all look like Smurfs,
and somehow the reference brought it back down to earth,
and then we had to choose a title for their end-of-year
anthology
and I realised how much of what they experienced
I chose not to see;
maybe I thought talking about racism
would be too hard for them and me,
with my white privilege
and their everyday code-switching.
But finally, we did it.
Aisha suggested the title *Do You Sleep in It?*
because that's what she'd once been asked,
then they had more stories
of stares and comments in the street.
I realised that without looking at these issues
their writing wasn't complete.
Aribah said, 'Don't judge us, we will surprise you;
the truth is really different from your stereotypical view.'
Urooj said, 'Modesty shouldn't make me strange.'
Aisha said, 'Some see it as a fashion statement,
but honestly it isn't.
It's a lot more than covering your hair;
the meaning is so deep your sanity might tear.'
Khadija said, 'Sometimes I wonder
why people judge me simply by what's on my head.
I've learned over time not to judge a curry by its smell,
so surely it's the same for people.'
In the end they voted to call their anthology
Into Our World
because they want people to know who they are:
not a cause of insurrection,
just young women who love writing
and Krispy Kremes and One Direction.
To be honest, many blokes find lots of women scary,
whether covered or naked, smooth or hairy.

I now look at why I wear what I do
and realise people judging women really isn't new,
so, yes, I have seen how they're dressed,
and I think to some degree
we're all oppressed
and free
and a hijab can be
both.

2.

To the man who sold me it
on a stall in Leeds open-air market,
who called me 'Sister',
it was a £4 tube of gem-encrusted pink fabric
he sold me, asking me why,
telling me not to worry if it made Muslims stare,
they would just be curious
about why a white woman was covering her hair.
I bowed my head, like a knight bowing for the Queen,
then entered the pink cocoon he held open
and emerged transformed.
In the Doc Martens shop and French Connection,
to the fundraisers from the Cats Protection League
and Guide Dogs for the Blind,
it was an invisibility cloak.
It was a lightning conductor for the odd bloke
and woman
who stared at me.
I think it made the woman on the till at Marks and Sparks
extra friendly
and it stole the usual smile from the Tesco cashier's face;
it made me realise that my village
is not a very diverse place.
I was more clothed,
but I felt exposed.
But for me a hijab was protection like
my fat
my wedding ring
my laughter

my hemline
my bra
my car.
It was a barrier like
my Northern vowels
getting to grips with sanitary towels
my laughter
my fat
my never wanting to be a mother
the fear I feel at blending into another.
It was ambiguous like
my blue hair
my friendly voice
my smile
my slightly bohemian sense of style.
It was a like a social obligation,
a uniform that shows you represent someone else,
like smiling to show you are safe,
like cheerful joining in to show you are prepared to fit in,
like waving at drivers of the same car.
It was dangerous like
my gender
my quick brain
my dysfunctional family
a mysterious stomach pain.
It was liberating like
my pots of hair colour
my quick brain
loving my husband and my dog
a vote
my own boat
a day without emails
my 'invisible' white skin.
It made me wary like
being thin
a street I've never walked down
a frown
a failing town
the sudden appearance of a rash.
It made me feel strong like

my thigh muscles
my quick brain
leaving my dysfunctional family
loving my husband and my dog.
It stood in for words like
a rhyme
a list
a greeting
small talk to fill the time.
It spoke for me for half a day;
I could not control what it would say.
It was a simile that was both like and not like,
a metaphor that goes beyond
one way to compare.
I can't yet cover in words
the effect of covering my hair.
What it was to realise
another way to be
simultaneously oppressed
and free.

PANDORA'S BOX

Commissioned by BBC Radio 5 Live on budget day 2017.

Three Northern girls' fates
rest on the contents
of the Chancellor's red box.
His budget unlocks
or closes off an alternative future.
Rewrites the story that could be written
for a post-Brexit Britain.
Imagine Sarah – who will invent
the world's cleanest ever bio-power,
but only if she gets out of that Gateshead tower
block, and can stop being her mum's carer
if she gets treated for chronic stress
on a cash-boosted NHS.
Imagine Aisha,
who would solve the Riemann hypothesis,
if she wasn't a late bloomer,
who'll fail a reinstated 11 plus
and become the fastest ever stock taker
at Stockport's Toys R Us.
Think of Georgia,
who would teach the founder of the most popular band
since the Beatles
to play guitar,
if only music degrees weren't too expensive
and far away,
and if her parents' shop in Kendal
didn't go bust after the hike
in small business rates.
These three aren't sole steerers
of their fates.
They're bulbs, not flowers;
they're pure potential.
Some social investment,
their growth would be exponential.
They wouldn't even become anything
that would annoy people,
like a female Doctor Who.
No pressure, Chancellor;

these unsung future heroines' hopes
for a world we can't yet imagine
rest on you.

CAROL AND THE WORKER BEES

She looked like a nice National Trust volunteer lady
who could be selling tea towels,
sat next to a nice National Trust man,
both eating their packed lunches,
and I tried not to look surprised
when it turned out they both maintained the steam engine
and water wheels. Got them going,
turned them off, repaired and oiled them as needed.

I remembered we're all a little bit sexist,
including me,
newly discovered Guilty Feminist.
I projected my sexism onto people of a couple
of centuries ago
and, fresh from learning about boy apprentices
learning maths and girl apprentices learning to sew,
and the way engineers were the elite of the mill
and always male,
I said to Carol that I presumed women didn't used to do that job.
She said that they weren't able to do it then,
and corrected herself to say
that they weren't thought capable of it.

I'd wanted to ask someone
about life-work balance
and mentioned some of the WI ladies
had included pictures of bees in their collage,
to show they were always busy bees.

Carol said they're a symbol of Manchester,
turn up on bins, bollards, everywhere,
because of how mills were a hive of industry.

I asked how long she'd volunteered
and she said since she retired.
I tried to look entirely unsurprised when she said
she and Ralph were both engineers.

Turns out he worked out
whether things could fly

and she ran the tests
to check whether they actually could.
'She told the pilots what to do,'
Ralph said gleefully.
'She's always liked telling people
what to do.'

I asked if it was harder,
working in a male-dominated industry,
and she said sometimes the blokes on the shopfloor
would thump their fists on the table
and say they'd been doing their job thirty years
and they weren't going to be told what to do
by a woman.
'I said that was fine,
but they still had to get on with it,'
said Carol mildly.

She said men would get the benefit of the doubt
they could do the job
until they made a mistake
but women had to prove they could do it.

I was going to ask how the heck
she got into that,
but bees were buzzing round my head
and a simile was starting to form
in my brain cells.

'Bees aren't supposed to be able to fly,
are they?' I asked them.
'Aerodynamically, I mean. But they can fly.'

Carol dipped and swooped imaginary bee wings,
and between them they said that recent experiments
had shown that bees bend them
so air forms pockets around them.

'Worker bees are all female,'
said Carol hesitantly

and my and Ralph's surprise made her
uncertain. We agreed it was unlikely
but didn't leap to Google
so we could enjoy the possibility longer.

She worked her way up, she said.
Turns out she started off as a typist.
'But she was rubbish at typing,'
said Ralph happily.
'She's still terrible at crosswords
and makes words up in Scrabble.'

They put her in the drawing room
and she was good at it,
kept being able to do what they asked her to do.
'Do you want to go flying?'
asked her boss one day,
and she ran test flights from the air.
'Telling everybody what to do,'
said Ralph again.
I thought sometimes teasing can be permission
as well as prohibition.

I suddenly realised
that flying aeroplanes that might not be able to fly
may be a bit scary,
but Carol talked about it
as if it was like trying out a new vacuum cleaner.

'There was that Nimrod that suddenly dropped
from fourteen thousand feet to four,'
she said so quietly I could hardly hear.
'Hydraulics going wrong,
sometimes the wires got put in the wrong way round

and that time we flew through a flock of birds
which would have downed us
if it had happened on take-off.'
They had to take away fifteen hundredweight
of dead birds
once they were back on solid ground.

Later, I look up worker bees
and she was right.
They are all female.
They don't have children,
but carry pollen
back and forth for the queen
and do all the other tasks in the hive
alongside the male drones,
but probably for lower pay.

I find that in 2005, scientists
attached small pieces of coloured glass
to bees' wings,
then set them flying in chambers
with most of the oxygen taken out
so they could monitor them.
They created barely perceptible mini-hurricanes
in their wake.

I think of all the men
who come up in the search results
when you Google 'the Industrial Revolution'.
I am full of glee
that this macho city
emblem celebrates a happily non-mothering lady bee.

Someone on my Facebook
says they're not really female,
because if their egg-producing pipes
are not used,
they're diverted to make poison instead.
I decide I like worker bees even more
and that they are definitely female.

Carol teasing and being teased by Ralph
as she keeps the power pumping through the mill,
laughing at the idea
of being interesting enough to put in a poem.

Worker bees,
who have had to keep on proving
they can fly.

SPINNING A YARN

Imagine
you're holding a thread
which is held by your mother,
then her mother,
then her mother,
double, treble, quadruple twisted ties,
back, back in a long line that stretches further than you can see.
Maybe you're all in a field.
Somehow it's not chaos,
somehow your nan's not distracted by the Yorkshire terrier
and your mum's not said anything mean about your hair
though mostly every alternate woman in my chain
would get on better with each other
than with the one right next to her.
Anyway, you're holding the end,
the thread's vibrating but it's just this frozen moment,
as if you're waiting for someone, maybe Bessie Greg,
to snap the lens shutter so you can go back to people who suit you,
your husband, your friends,
this is sort of an obligation, sort of a privilege,
this moment,
making the chain, of women you'll still mostly never name,
as they stretch into the horizon's edge
and you're all worried it will rain,
but you're hearing fragments of chatter,
that school Granny Sair'ann ran,
how a younger Auntie Ann became a bursar,
these women who are not on an official record,
who didn't chuck themselves under a horse,
but who managed to steer their own course
through the things they were told they couldn't do,
shouldn't do. They made it work.
They weren't allowed strategies,
they couldn't shuffle soldiers
across maps, piece up and rearrange continents,
but they all had tactics,
making the best of what they had,
the day-to-day resistances and choices,
and even though we can't see their faces
or hear their voices,

you hold that thread that they've all spun,
and still the looms are clacking on,
the threads are criss-crossing with other chains,
from women written out of history,
with ones who shouted loudly.
The more twists a thread is given,
the stronger it becomes.
Black threads, white threads,
ones that got lost and trampled in the dirt
for years,
but at this moment it's making a double helix
down your maternal line,
then springs back,
echoes of thunderous looms,
the shuttle's clack,
you're holding it, just this one thread
in the great weave of history.
Will you keep to the old pattern
or start a new one?
Lose the weft, keep the warp?
Find new materials,
a different yarn to spin?
Can you drop that thread altogether,
take up ones from another kin?
These choices
which are not completely yours
and not completely not.
Take this moment
while you can
to throw a nod of recognition
to the thread holders down the line,
then it's yours. Begin.

THE SOUVENIRISTS OF QUARRY BANK MILL, 2117

Museum visitors dress in the early twenty-first century
'National Trust' fleeces and denims,
to experience what it was like
to walk around in clothes.
If you are experiencing female gender
you will have to wear undergarments on both halves
of your body, and slightly less comfortable jeans.
An audio-visual guide can be downloaded
to the chip inside your brain,
where you can see, in 3D, Quarry Bank Mill
as a working mill, then museum and now museum of a museum.
   Meta.
At the end of the tour you will be able to upload your vote
as to which of these incarnations you think is better.

Our memory bots will escort you round the mill
and demonstrate
the looms and industrial machinery,
as the 'National Trust' memory workers
used to do in 2017.
They have been downloaded
with the actual memories
and voices of humans
who worked at Quarry Bank at the time.

For example, John, who will say,
'I am the robot version of myself.
I'm sure the management think this one is better.'
You will note the dry humour
of the volunteers,
and the authentic hairiness of some of their ears.

Jess, who felt that places had an essence
that could be captured in their objects
and was intrigued by cogs, gears, pulleys
and how an engine, like a team,
cannot function if something is missing.

Emma, another female human, who recognised
that tools have personalities,
and said she got on well with the finisher carding machine,
but the draw frame didn't like her.

You will also be able to visit our Robot-Slave exhibition
which is a result of a Global Earth Council collaboration
between robot and human historians
exploring the cultural links
between the concept of the 'worker' and the 'robot'.

We have removed most of the aeroplane noise from the sky
using our special sound shield.
We play rare early twenty-first century sounds such as bird noises
and wind blowing grass across the fields.

You will experience using physical money
in the 'National Trust' café
and enjoy historical treats specific to 2017 including
white bread sandwiches
and a kind of biscuit-cake known as a scone.
Health nanobots will be available to cleanse
your digestive system afterwards.
You will be able to hear long-gone
animals such as the bee and smell extinct flowers
such as the rhododendron.

Many of the staff and volunteers
showed a deep emotional attachment to Quarry Bank
and will talk to you about being pulled
there by magic, causing them to work for cheap or free.
This demonstrates the unusual spiritual beliefs
of early twenty-first century late capitalism
which also extend to a faith
in the reviving power of the tannin-and-caffeine-filled drink
known as 'a nice cup of tea',
which you will be fed every hour during your visit
for maximum authenticity.

Now we have reached the singularity,
the view that all matter, organic and inorganic,
strives towards reaching its fullest expression
is gaining ground. Do not worry; there will be more scones, tea
and an interpretive holographic, poetic dance element to ensure
you are able to digest
these difficult ideas.

STONEWALL

She stares straight down the camera lens,
as if daring the photographer to make her stay
in the nineteenth century.
The front row girls sit,
hands folded neatly in laps;
the rest of the back row
stand clasping their hands
behind their backs or at their sides,
shrinking to close the gaps between them,
faces blank as bricks.
She is the only one not wearing a white apron.
The only one with a clenched fist on her hip,
jaw set, eyes unflinching,
her other hand planted on the girl in front's shoulder
as if she's about to confer a medal.
Maybe she would become Bella Pepper,
who was a bit of a character
according to the man they taped remembering Styal.
Or maybe she would become the Nancy Johnson
they nicknamed Stonewall Jackson
after the American Civil War hero
she channelled while pioneering the village's co-op,
though her role in that would go unwritten.
Maybe she knew her name would drop from history
like a lost battle.
Maybe people alive today
are walking round Styal or New York or Glasgow
wearing her features.
Maybe there's a nativity Mary
with her eyebrows,
clonking Joseph with a toy sheep
while looking defiantly down the barrel
of somebody's overused video camera.
Someone with her nose
who's not massively impressed
they called her 'feisty' on local telly
just for holding banners.
You wouldn't want to tell her
that the gormless blokes
flanking the aproned girls

would still be the only ones we can name.
Look again, keep looking.
She's still there
waiting for the flash
daring you
not to look away.

LEADING THE POWER VOLUNTEERS

Another man is asking Jess
if she has a team of men
to fix the machines for her.
His wife points out
that Jess is holding
a massive spanner
and it looks like
she's not afraid
to use it.

ONE POSITION IN WHICH THEY FELT RESTRICTED, ONE POSITION IN WHICH THEY FELT FREE

For Esther, it was crouching under clacking looms
retrieving bits of roving,
an ache in her chest when she thought of home.
It was rushing past the overlooker at the door,
shouting she won't be shut up
with Mrs Timperley's body
no matter how much they punish her for the crime.

For Bessie, it was being made to practise
walking with a book on her head, holding herself in
like the lady she never wanted to be.
It was lining up a shot
in her camera lens, then watching the image emerge
from silver nitrate
like a celebrated man's map outline.

For Ann, it was bending in the hearth at dawn,
with red and white fingers and sore knees,
to set a fire for somebody else's warmth.
It was the loud then quiet of the grand organ
moving her back and forth
like a clock about to chime.

For Elizabeth, it was standing graveside
in the black crepe dress,
when she already felt like a dammed-up beck.
It was looking up at the glass house ceiling
installed by her workers,
blinking at refracting prisms of spring sunshine.

For Mary, it was shivering in bed while bells
and hooves and the voice telling her she is wicked
pounded her head.
It was running from room to room
when she arrived home,
pink as the gardens at rhododendron time.

For Margaret, it was headaches clouding her vision
as she pieced cotton on moving carriages so quickly
you couldn't see the join.
It was walking up and down the machines
she oversaw,
power from the drive shaft
flowing straight through her spine.

BRADFORD BECK

This poem inadvertently inspired me to set up the Poets and Spoken Word Artists' Network (now the Poetry and Spoken Word Group of the union the Society of Authors) with Tamar Yoseloff, after Bradford Council made a call-out for poets to submit poems for an unpaid commission to put on stones in the city centre.

Forgotten river, potent as a family secret.
Liquid arteries pulse under city traffic.
Origin of this city's name, a hidden tonic.
Water woven into a patchwork quilt of culverts.
Skeletal waterway, revived by rain.
Underground channels chalk through cathedral chambers
Neglected for centuries, dark as the Styx.
Drained by toil, resting on a mossy bed of millstone grit.
Elixir to itself, amniotic stream.
Remembering light, shaley water's dream.
Subterranean worker who never clocked off.
Old wounds heal under a fireclay sarcophagus.
Life replenishes, bouldered funnels fill.
Escaping from time's tunnels, trout swim, kingfishers fly.
Sea-bound, breaking from the Aire to echo the sky.

OTHER PEOPLE'S BAGGAGE

It's somewhere England keeps on dreaming
its progressiveness has never died,
or it's a festival that's lost its meaning,
middle-aged and gentrified.

It's not as good as it used to be
or it's better than it's ever been.
It's somewhere to see things in a whole new light
or just somewhere to be seen.

You don't go there if you want to be free
or it lets you be whoever you are.
It's where everyone's equal with mud on their feet
or the corporate culture has gone too far.

We used to go there to escape The Man
and now we're worried that he's there,
or it's still a place to explore an ideal world
and find new ways to make it fair.

It's a posh prison camp, the Kate Moss show,
it's a place to flog your brand
or it's a community of exploration
which can inspire you to take a stand.

It's a farmer's visionary gift,
a jewel for the nation,
or a symbol of selling out,
a site of working-class alienation.

It's too expensive and corporate,
I'm fed up with all that shit,
or it's a place for beautiful pleasures
where the alternative flame's still lit.

It's too multiple for simple labels,
I suspect I'll find it's all of them and none,
but I don't want to be burdened
with other people's baggage
before my packing has even begun.

PACKING LIST

I have my wellies,
a Pac-a-Mac,
sunscreen and a brolly.
I've got some ear plugs,
a plastic bowl,
wet wipes and a trolley.
I've got a tent and my ticket,
a camera and dry hand gel;
will I need a solar shower
and an extra ground sheet as well?
Should I bring a quick-dry towel,
a stove and a mosquito net?
I haven't got a cafetière
or an antimacassar yet.
I think I'll need some crutches,
a harmonica and a sheep,
a pasta maker,
a belly button defluffer,
and a lullaby to help me sleep.
A mind-expander,
a rhyme for 'orange',
my soul and a steady gaze,
some questionless answers,
a left brain-trancer
and a year of extra days.
Pandora's box,
some anti-matter
and the sound of the earth
as it's turning,
fathomless silence,
Fermat's Last Theorem,
and my generation's unsaid yearning.
The meaning of life,
the horror of it all
and the truth that will finally save us.
I hope I can fit all that in
my bag
'cause I'm getting there
on the bus.

GLASTONBURY 3013

The Rolling Stones have just played the Pyramid Stage
for the first time since they were defrosted.
It's thirty-five degrees in the shade,
the solar deflection canopies are decorated
with outline maps of Britain before the Great Flood of 2085
(a record year for Glastonbury poncho sellers).
The price of grass has soared. Meadow grass.
People photograph Worthy Farm's carefully cultivated patches
on their retina-cams.
Their prize-winning herd of milking camels
give rides from the Chris Moyles stage to the Green Fields.
A man with an icicle-white beard and a Greenpeace T-shirt
shows archive footage
from 2013: close-ups of Paula the polar bear's fur, the Arctic
Dome.
Says, 'Back then, we showered you with snow,
emphasised the short window
to save the Arctic, well…' He turns out his hands,
gestures to the yellow sky.
'We told you so.'

BILLY BRAGG'S BEARD

Billy Bragg's beard bristles at inequality,
has got fascism by the short and curlies.
Billy Bragg's beard is not red, but it should be.
It is strongest on the far left.
Well-travelled whiskers
which don't believe in stopping close shaves and rash moments.
Billy Bragg's beard is all about active growth and change.
Shows that a small group of committed hairs
can change the face of man.
Billy Bragg's beard has been accused of going country,
owes a debt to Woody Guthrie.
Billy Bragg's beard will frame direct words until justice wins
and (he says) hides a multitude of chins.

SIMON'S SEWAGE

You can download all the footage,
stream the bands non-stop,
but you've not really experienced Glastonbury
without a long poo drop

and your Glastonbury Festival
will not have been complete
until you perfect your hover
above that fragrant toilet seat.

The breeze on your nether regions
offers a peculiar kind of bliss
and if you visit in the middle of the night
you won't have to glimpse the deep abyss.

I must confess, I've access
to some posher kinds of loo;
they flush recycled water
that's been dyed a chemical blue.

I spoke to Simon, who empties them;
he says they smell quite nice,
though you wouldn't want to drink the water
by the time it's been round twice.

Normally he's a farmer,
but can turn his hand to a pipe and a mop.
He says he enjoys meeting people,
once he's pumped away their plop.

I asked him for the worst sight he'd ever encountered;
he referred to the medics' tent.
I thought he was going to reveal the aftermath
of some huge accident.

But he said the medics' turds are massive,
the biggest he's ever seen
He can only think it's their healthy diet,
the effects of rice and bean.

I know sludging through the sewage
is not to everybody's taste,
but the sheer scale of this event
means we're cheek by jowl with waste.

No poet can ever hope to convey
the Glastonbury toilet whiff;
you'll just have to scent it for yourself
or wait 'til the Beeb does scratch-and-sniff.

MICK JAGGER'S YURT

He can watch Glasto on a plasma telly,
there's steaming showers
if things get smelly,
but there's not a single speck of dirt
in Mick Jagger's yurt.

There's a chef, a pool,
a helipad,
a jester ready if he gets sad,
and supermodels fight to flirt
in Mick Jagger's yurt.

A string quartet lulls him to sleep,
a jumper's spun
from his personal sheep,
the security guards are never curt
in Mick Jagger's yurt.

The ceiling's studded with diamonds,
there's a dodo feather quilt,
a secret tunnel to Martinique
has been especially built,
noble gases remain inert
in Mick Jagger's yurt.

The air's so pure your lungs expand,
there's a 6G signal
pumped in by hand,
Keith Richards' lumbago doesn't hurt
in Mick Jagger's yurt.

It's not ordinary life he wants to dodge,
it's just Glastonbury's not got
a Travelodge,
but even Bono would sell his shirt
to sleep in Mick Jagger's yurt.

LIFEBOAT

Written and performed with the students of South Shields Community College for BBC1's (live) broadcast of the Great North Passion in 2014.

I think I'm kind of kind,
but like most of us I'm somewhere in between
the saintly giving of Mother Theresa
and the bumbling awkwardness of Mr Bean.

Your haircut makes me cringe.
Your phone is so old!
Hashtag
Kindness of Strangers

see Twitter and Galilee
or head to Ocean Road, South Shields,
for a day out by the sea!

Fish and chips and curry,
Indian, Chinese and Thai,
anything you want to eat
is here for you to buy.
Ice creams!
Made by Minchella's all the way from Italy.
People came from all over the world to live here
and, mostly, they get on.
Thirteen flavours of us.

The first ever lifeboat design,
saved a thousand from the Tyne,
was saved in turn by volunteers,
who wiped away the years
until it was bright blue and white
as the prom on a sunny day.

The seagulls pinch your pasty,
nick your chips,
sit on your head,
a clucking army pecking bits of bread.
Haway, the fair!

Dodgems, waltzers, a slide,
a rollercoaster, the party bus.
Life is a journey, so come with us,
all the way from the Tyne Bridge.
The Great North Run!
Drummers thump heartbeats in time with the runners,
photos of loved ones on their backs.

I had no breath, I'd gone puce,
my knees were weak, my lungs no use,
but the crowd gave me
water!
Jelly babies!
The will to carry on!

Give someone a lift if they break down
(but what if they're a psychopath?),
present a random person with a bunch of flowers
(but what if they just laugh?),
help an old person when they fall over
(but what if you're not medically trained?).

Burly blokes on boats
is just one kind of brave,
but stick your neck out for others,
it's your own life you will save.

Your hair is lush.
Let's give your car a push.
You don't even need make-up.
Do you want a hand with that shopping?
You smell of strawberries.

We will be your lifeboat
and come to your rescue.
We will bring it back to *you*
so you can't forget.

Treat others the way you want to be tret.
Treat others the way you want to be tret.

LISTEN TO WHAT THEY KNOW

BBC-commissioned poem for the Hartlepool First World War Bombardment Memorial in 2014, by Kate Fox and the students of Dyke House School.

Crackling voices through the static.
Memories of a hundred years ago
transmit stories which must not die;
we will be their radio.

Mary makes a cup of tea.
Thunder is coming from the sea.
Mary gets ready for her school day.
A storm is on the way.
Thomas watches from the top of the hill.
Battleships set their sights to kill.

Can you hear the guns?
They're coming.
Come on, get away.
There's no such thing as running out the door,
We are going to

STAY.

Fear like screams that make you scream more,
running feet make you run for the cellar or the door.

PANIC.

Thomas watches smoke rise from a rooftop;
will the whistling shells ever stop?

Mary comes to and crawls outside.
Soldiers carry her to help – she thought she had died.

Crackling voices through the static.
Memories of a hundred years ago
transmit stories which must not die;
we will be their radio.

A boy, our age, goes to the shop and
never
comes
back.
His mother goes to find him and
never
comes
back.
After forty-five long minutes, the ships
turn
back.

Silence.
Choking dust in the grey.
Over a hundred people
did not finish the day.

Flattened.   Shattered.   Collapsed.
It's as if the world has ended.
Walls can be rebuilt, roofs can be mended

but
hearts,
trust,
safety…

Waking in the middle of the night
dreaming you are being buried alive.
Storms make you sprint for the cellar,
even though you managed to survive.

But hope is stronger than fear,
especially at this time of year.

Hope is a new view over the old sea,
hope is the smell of a Christmas tree.
Hope is a future that you dare to see,
it's a new generation, alive and free.

Hope is opening doors on your advent calendar,

it's wanting your favourite *X Factor* contestant to get through,
it's a party, it's a bridge, it's wrapping paper,
it's the sun coming up over Seaton Carew.

It's a football truce between warring sides,
it's the school bell at the end of the day,
it's washing powder and snow on your tongue,
it is the song of the mockingjay.

It's a rebuilt church ringing out a call,
it's a gift given with no hope of return,
it's the belief you will win and the fighting will stop,
it's the faith human beings will finally learn.

Crackling voices through the static.
Memories of a hundred years ago
transmit stories which must not die.
Waves hit the headland like an echo.

Listen to what they know.
Listen to what they know.
Listen to what they know.

PAPER TOWN

With all Edinburgh's discarded flyers
you could build a whole other city:
printed trees, cardboard houses, paper spires.
Glossy in the sunshine,
not so good during rain or fires.

A FRINGE PERFORMER'S FIRST DAY AT THE FRINGE

You've got possession of
your new office
for about an hour a day.
People will come and watch you work,
if you're lucky.
You're on very variable pay.
Sometimes, when you're at the office,
there are hecklers.
Your parents think this job
means you're pretty feckless.
In this office there'd be nothing crueller
than no one talking about you
round the water cooler.
You've got less than a month
to get that promotion.
No pressure.
If you're lucky maybe there'll be
an office romance.
No matter how hard things get,
don't try the David Brent dance.

FRINGE PIMP

My husband sells me on the street.
He is the perfect spouse.
When he's not pimping me to strangers
he's papering the house.
He takes care of washing, cooking
and sorting out the bills
and spends the month letting others benefit
from my oral skills.

HECKLER

I just want to join in,
be in a double act,
I'll be the Morecambe to your Wise,
just let me interact.
I'll shout out the end of your joke,
tell you what I had for tea,
it shouldn't just be about you,
it could also be about me.
I'll be your unpaid gag writer,
you don't need to ask me twice.
'Get off,' 'Get your tits out,' 'Get on with it,'
I'm just offering some advice.
I don't even need a microphone,
I'm loud enough to shout.
I know you were enjoying my contribution
until those bouncers threw me out…

OPTIMISM

I need several stars
for my career to thrive.
Yesterday I got two and then three;
hurrah, that makes five!

FRINGE FATIGUE HAIKU

By show twenty-two,
not even got the strength to
finish my fringe hai…

TITANIC

Another anniversary, another fuss,
another reason to feel smug
that you're on the bus.
Another film, another song,
Celine Dion warbling on,
Strictly's Len on telly to relive it,
every turbine, every rivet.
When they say 'commemorate',
it seems they actually meant
'let's celebrate' –
as if programme makers
are really thinking
it was fantastic

apart from the sinking.

CONSERVATIVE VALENTINE POEM TO THE NORTH-EAST

Flood warnings are red.
Tories are blue.
Money is no object,
we know that is true.
The North-East is red,
the South-East is blue,
so we won't be
spending it on you.

THE NEW CHARTER

Another commission for Radio 3's The Verb *– with the trees
voiced by Beccy Owen's Pop-Up Choir. There are calls for a
new version of the 1217 Forest Charter.*

In our n**ew** charter
for forests, people and trees,
we are pleased to celebrate
trees' role as continuing providers
of ecological services.
We **do** hope their relationship
with us, their clients,
can lead to a productive alliance
for us all, from first bud to leaf fall,
from germination to final termination,
through shedding, k**not**ting
and burning.
With, of course, an **onus**
on forest managers to keep efficiency
at a maximum throughout the seasons' turning.

TREES:
You do not own us.
You do not own us.

The trees' responsibilities include:
carbon storage and removal,
allowing shade,
new ultra-tough timbers and biomass energy
to be made.
Furniture and cellulose production,
noise and flood reduction.
Cleansing of water and soil,
substitution for coal and oil,
providing bird, animal and insect housing,
migration corridors,
food and fuel,
hiding ugly buildings and keeping them cool.
Allowing saunas to be built and fired.
Plus producing paper, Christmas decoration,

national myths and leisure opportunities
as required.

We see trees as our companion vegetation
and promise we **will** assist their ongoing regeneration,
promote genetic diversity and other best practice
so they don't die **out**
because of pathogens and pests.
We will conserve the planet,
so we can **live** in harmony with nature
and help **you** enjoy the bounty of it.

TREES:
We will outlive you.
We will outlive you.

Forests allow obese citizens
to use them as gyms,
let agoraphobic chickens
wander freely in arboreal shelter
producing more eggs,
encourage cyclists and children
to **us**e their legs,
commuters to recover from **work** stress
by breathing fresh air
and watching dark skies and Rick Astley concerts.
For those unimpressed **with** the thought
of too much nature,
we have created Gruffalo trails,
souvenir shops and clear paths so **you** will **not**
ever feel too far from civilisation.
Our **fo**rests are a safe place
for **you** to counter modern life's alienation.

TREES:
Let us work with you, not for you.
Let us work with you, not for you.

We are working to make trees
genetically modified for our needs,

so they can provide a resilient
solution-focused resource,
provide measurable fruit and seed based outcomes,
grow quickly, **live** productively, shed slickly,
be adaptable, yet predictable,
insured for all human cont**act**,
amenable to **a** zero-hours contract,
responsive to **different** circumstances as they arise,
flexible about working s**pace**s,
able to think out of boxes and blue skies.

TREES:
We live at a different pace
We live at a different pace

Everyone should plant a tree.
Everyone should cut one down.
Oak trees were planted
to power Britain's navy
but used as pit props
during the Industrial Revolution.
Along with birch,
hazel, pine,
alder, elm and lime,
the oak is one of our native trees.
We came to this country as refugees,
seeding ahead of the ice sheet
over eight thousand years ago.
They symbolise so much.
We are as real as you.
Stability in an uncertain world.
An ash tree can be bisexual,
a hermaphrodite or change sex entirely,
whatever it needs
to spread its seeds.
Beautiful **(useful)**, solid **(mutable)**, ancient **(ageless)**.
There for everyone.
We cannot be owned.

THEY'RE CLOSING THE UNICORNS

Dear Citizens,

We're being very honest with you here. We just can't afford to feed all the city unicorns anymore. We want to, believe us, we do, but central government haven't given us enough money because the South's spending it all on ponies. I know we've all appreciated the joy and wonder unicorns have brought to us all since we introduced them. The ineffable sense of transcendence we all get when we see a flick of a white tail and a tilt of an exquisitely turned spiral horn. That day the herd ran amok in Primark and showed us all the true meaning of wilderness confronting consumer culture. The way we attract external investment with pictures of our amazing retail and leisure opportunities plus photos of herds of wild unicorns sweeping majestically across the convenient car parks.

But the government doesn't really give a toss about that stuff. They're Tories, after all. So, to help us make our case for more money, could we do it in language they do understand? Please, please tell us the impact fewer unicorns will make on your life and wellbeing. What will it do to the ecosystem if they disappear from your neighbourhood? Might it create particular social and economic consequences or hardship if the packs are eradicated from specific areas? We will be maintaining a central unicorn park and are relieved to say 95% of the population will still live within 1.5 miles of a unicorn, but we know it won't be the same.

This might also be the time to let you know that our whole relationship with you, citizen to council, is changing because of how Eric Pickles would rather we didn't exist at all and wants to destroy us like he destroys a plate pie. We need you to be more involved. Let us know what you think, help out with community solutions. Unfortunately, we're having to tell you a massive paradigm-shifting thing like that in the middle of documents you probably don't read. It's a bit like including a Dear John letter in the middle of your gas bill. Perhaps we should paint this message on the side of unicorns!

Anyhoo, look at our occasionally conversational language and chummy webchats. We are trying. Here's a reiteration of the most important bit of what we've said. It's dying kids or unicorns – you choose, but it's not our fault.

Also – please can you think of any ways we can come together and help? Maybe have community unicorn feeding schedules, adopt a unicorn, even sponsor a unicorn? ('Bernard's Bras Give You the Horn!' etc., real opportunities there.) Could schools keep some? Perhaps volunteers could have them in their allotments. It's only turnips that make them rampage. We'll provide start-up costs. I know none of us want to lose the benefits of our city's amazing unicorns. Don't forget to be angry at central government. And honestly – HELP!

Yours,
The Council

Dear the Council,

Save our unicorns! Or we'll tell the *Guardian* that you're culling them all in a big Boxing Day hunt. Please find attached hundreds of personal testimonies about the importance of unicorns in our lives. You philistines. We know you never liked them anyway.

The Writers

P.S. Some famous authors, singers and Cheryl Cole have also written to the papers about their love of unicorns. You'll be sorry.

WOMANIFESTO

Written after a 'think-in' planning meeting for Hull's Women of the World festival, 2017, and reflecting what the women of the city want for the future.

'Manifesto' means to make public,
'manifest' means to make clear,
this womanifesto declares it's on the march,
it's everywhere and it is here.

It's showing up, it's showing off,
it's not apologetic or dull,
it has something for everyone
but it was birthed in Hull.

It will lead but not get called 'bossy'
or told it's good 'for a girl'.
It will be proclaimed in school assemblies,
it will score goals, hit wickets and curl.

It will be written while we queue for the loo,
but it will ask for potty parity.
It will embrace chaos and mess,
and womansplain with reason and clarity

It will have a million different ways
of being beautiful,
not just the ones the magazines say.
It will challenge gender binaries
and demand equal pay.

It will be stamped 'Made in Hull',
it will let hidden places and people shine,
it will remember the headscarf revolutionaries,
it will be up for having a good time.

It will be graffitied on city hall walls
where too many men in suits make the decisions.
It will be proud of Hull's fourteen female mayors,
and challenge history's revisions.

It will come up from the grass roots
and it will go on tour,
it can have what London has
and it can have something more.
It will be scientific and astronomical,
technological and mathematic;
when it shows its feelings
it won't get told it's being 'dramatic'.

It will travel the world,
and it will know the value of home,
it won't stay in and do the housework,
it will hold out a hand to those who battle alone.

It will build a wall against sexists – and Trump –
from bricks of solidarity, mockery and hope.
It will Tweet and protest and strike,
celebrate a female Doctor Who, president and pope!

It will be sung from the centre
and shouted from poverty's edge,
it will ask organisations benefiting from Hull 17
to make an equality pledge.

It will be blazoned across the sky,
it will smash the glass ceiling
and look down from above,
it will be smiley – if it wants to,
but it won't 'cheer up, love'.

It will be gobby and nebby and loud,
it will stand together for a cause,
it will be dangerous and laughing and proud,
it will be our womanifesto – and yours.

So write it across a banner,
rhyme it, engrave it, say it, give it,
sing it, craft it, play it,
but most importantly live it.

THE SUBSTITUTION

I worked with graphic artist Tommy Anderson to tell the stories of six very different Gateshead residents for an exhibition Gateshead Library agreed to put on in May 2015. We got them to write and to do art with us. Their poems remain theirs, but these are two responses to them. 'The Substitution' is for Gateshead's now former arts chaplain Jim Craig, who talked about the power of brokenness in his work and in art. 'Alice' comes from the work of Molly, a Gateshead teenager who found release in this project when her creativity was stifled in so many ways in other places. The 'Annie, Eric, Helen, Jim, Molly, Tommy' exhibition made me even more determined to speak with people, not for them.

Theseus feels he has no choice
but to follow the thread
into the labyrinth.

Especially when we ask him,
'Are you insured?
Have you done a risk assessment?'

Or say,
'Minotaurs are dangerous, you know,
you'll get a disease,
you'll pick up fleas.'

We question,
'What's the point?
Do you know where you're going?
Isn't there a better signposted path
you could be following?'

Theseus grasps the yarn
while we fuss.

Tempted to point out
he is only doing this
on behalf of all the rest of us.

ALICE

There are long corridors,
square rooms and rectangular desks
where they want you to get by without pictures
or conversations.

The signposts point two ways at once
and the white rabbit rings a bell at regular intervals
to tell you that you were already too late
by about forty years.

Screens flash up instructions for you to drink and eat,
but as soon as you pluck the currants one by one
with hesitant fingers,
they tell you that you are too big,
then too small
to reach the key.

Don't see what you eat
or eat what you see,
and both ravens and writing desks are so last year.

A virtual grin made of commas
lingers in the air.

Somebody put caterpillars
in the Sensory Garden,
though the mushrooms were banned.

The Mad Hatter's on a zero-hours contract
and the Queen hands out sanctions
like sentences,
to all those who have never played croquet.

You hold a hand of cards
for a game you've never been taught.

The mock turtle showers you
with 'the best that's ever been said and thought',

which you brush off
as it turns into a pile of dead leaves.

BRAVE NEW WORDS

A commission for the opening of Billingham's new library in 2015.

Billa's people first uttered Brave New Words
in the shadow of the Eston Hills,
laying the foundations for this word hoard.
Leaves turned to the sun, became the way our culture's stored
in alphabetical and numerical order, shaping chaos.
Now noughts and ones, shelves and pages
Grow together and bind the ages.
House of books and dreams,
a window on to the town
mirrors families in love and loss.
Library. Portal to new worlds,
imagination generator, time machine, kaleidoscope,
beacon of hope, information superhighway.
Regeneration towers rise and fall, our shared stories renew:
Austen's heroines to jet propulsion, Stephen King to zoo,
reminders of who you are and who you can be,
your mind opened, connected, free.

Free. Connected. Open your mind
to who you can be. Who you are. You are reminded
of Austen, jets, zoos and kings.
Stories renewed and shared, rising, towering, falling.
Superhighway information, hopeful beacon,
kaleidoscope, time generator, imagination machine.
New world portal. Library.
Families. Love and loss. A mirror
to the town. A window
full of dreams. A book of houses.
Bound together as ages grow.
Shelved ones, sought pages
chaos shaped, by order of alphabet and number.
Stored cultures, the way the sun became leaves –
hoarding the layers and foundations of words
Eston Hills foreshadowed,
the words 'brave', and 'new'. Uttering first – 'Billa's people.'

WE THOUGHT THERE'D BE MORE PEOPLE

Dedicated to my dedicated fellow workers in poem, gig promoters and audiences who come out to see live poetry.

We thought there'd be more people,
we don't know where they've gone,
we were packed out last week
when we had the stripper on.

We thought there'd be more people
but it's raining, sunny, snowing, dark,
they must be at the footie, watching *Corrie*,
barbecuing in the park.

We thought there'd be more people,
you deserve more, there's no doubt;
if we had six more months to advertise
I'm sure we'd have sold out.

We thought there'd be more people,
we hope that you don't mind,
we thought there'd be more people,
this venue's hard to find.

We thought there'd be more people,
they promised they would come,
at least I'm here and you're here,
and the venue owner's Mum.

We thought there'd be more people,
they must have got lost along the way,
we thought there'd be more people
but it's always hard to say.

We thought there'd be more people
and walk-ups at the door,
we thought there'd be more people
but it's Shakin' Stevens' farewell tour.

We thought there'd be more people

but there's been a lot of flu about,
we thought there'd be more people
but they're not used to coming out.
We thought there'd be more people
but no one can afford a ticket,
we thought there'd be more people,
we're competing with the cricket.

We thought there'd be more people,
the info went out quite late,
we thought there'd be more people,
we should have picked the other date.

We thought there'd be more people –
that's not us being boasters,
perhaps next time we'll make some flyers
or maybe even posters.

We thought there'd be more people,
we booked the biggest room
because the *Guardian* did an article
about the Poetry Boom.

We thought there'd be more people
but you're no Kate Tempest or Cooper Clarke;
still, like black cats, your audience
will look similar in the dark.

We thought there'd be more people,
well, at least some more than three.
But you're lucky there's anyone here at all,
since you're doing poetry.

ACKNOWLEDGEMENTS

Thank you to all the organisations who commissioned these poems and the wonderful people I collaborated with and spoke to in all my researches.